Recognising and Removing the
3 Mental Barriers to
High Performance and Happiness

Anthony Bonnici

www.brainblinkers.com
www.movemountains.com.au

Brain Blinkers

Illustrations by Lizzy Simunovic.

ISBN: 9781742840314 (pbk.)

Published by Book Pal
www.bookpal.com.au

Contents

For my family:
Samuel, Milan, Isabella, William
and my beautiful wife Julie.

With so much love and appreciation for what
you do for me, where we have been, and where
we are going.

INTRODUCTION

She was beaming, but her eyes were wet.

It was September 2007 and Move Mountains – my professional heart and soul, the company I started in 2005 – had been going for a bit over two years. I was presenting my cornerstone keynote at the conference for the Australian Institute of Office Professionals (AIOP).

I closed my talk, thanked the audience, and they kindly applauded. All of them then got up for morning tea, and amidst the hustle and bustle of two hundred attendees, mainly women, chatting and shuffling out of the room, a number of delegates stayed behind to share a thought with me.

"Thanks so much. I really enjoyed it." "That was great. Is this your full time job?""Really loved the story about the Ford vs. Holden – you described my Dad!"

She was the last in line. Something had clearly clicked for her, and I figured that by virtue of the fact that she was smiling, it was "positive."

As the second to last lady left the line, I felt compelled to preface our conversation. *"Is everything alright?"* I asked with a genuinely concerned tone.

"Yes fine thank you. I won't tell you why but you really struck a chord with me today," she said.
"I'm honoured, and thanks for sharing that with me." I replied.

"My pleasure" she responded. *"So, do you have a book that I can buy?"*

I stood there perplexed. Books were what famous people do. Surely, she was confusing me with someone else.

"Ah, no, well um, not yet anyway," was my response: all class.

"Well, can you promise me that you will write one?" she pleaded.

I smiled, thinking she was having me on, but the look on her face said otherwise. So I said *"Yes."*

This book is the result of that promise from three years ago.

If you are looking for a psychological or motivational almanac, then put the book down now. There are hundreds of more illustrious souls who have attempted to do just that – some successfully, others not so successfully. You will find some excellent further reading on these topics later in this book.

I wrote this book as a way of condensing and documenting the thoughts, theories, stories and tools that have helped me create my life, and my company. Writing this book helped me clarify why I enjoyed being a sales manager earlier in my career, and helped me understand what I was actually doing in my role as a manager to affect change in the people who reported to me. It is a personal perspective on an ancient and mostly unanswered challenge: how can we change our behaviour, our output, and our actions?

In researching the content for Brain Blinkers – which, back in 2007, had the very catchy title of "Finding the Mental Barriers that Stop Us Doing Well" – I have obviously been affected and influenced by the fields of behavioural and organisational psychology, but also opened my mind to the somewhat more controversial areas of Neurolinguistic Programming (NLP) and hypnosis. I purposefully chose to use tools and theories from both the conscious and subconscious or unconscious perspectives of this hotly debated topic, as I believe, like most things in life, that the truth lies somewhere in the middle. This book does not follow one way or the other: it is not just a cognitive behavioural approach, nor is it simply an NLP approach. It is a hybrid, and I know the purists will be fuming. I could not care less – this book is a personal perspective, so as John Lennon put it, "whatever gets you through the night."

In sharing Brain Blinkers with over 10,000 people in three continents over the past five years, I know that the content appeals to a broad variety of people and situations. This book will resonate for the following types of people:

- The sales person who feels like they cannot make an impact
- The middle manager who feels her head pressing against the "glass ceiling"
- The career man who cannot understand why he is not progressing
- The singer who knows they can sing but never feels confident
- The student who feels pressured into a career or educational path
- The leader who doubts their ability to lead

- The checkout operator who does not feel they deserve anything better
- The mother of two wondering why she is parenting just like her mother, when she did not want it to work out that way
- The person who always freaks out when asked to speak in front of group
- The teenager playing sport on a Saturday who just cannot get the voices of his parents out of his head
- The individual who believes "how I am is how I am," and does not believe in the possibility of change, even if they wanted to.

This book means nothing if nothing changes for you. Its style and content is purposefully brief in order to facilitate note taking and reflection. By far the most important part of the book are the final few pages in which you document what you are going to do about your Brain Blinkers. It is, after all, a journey of self-awareness.

Like I did for the beaming lady at the AIOP conference in 2007, promise you will do something, and then do it.

Chapter 1: Brain Blinkers?

"Well, it's like a blinker on the brain..."

I needed to clear my head. I had so much going on, the business was growing and yet I felt uncomfortable about the major part of my heart-and-soul keynote presentation because it simply was not singing.

Blessed with parents who are overly eager to be with our four young children, I planned to go for a run with Julie around one of Sydney's famous jogging tracks – the Bay Run, an excellent seven-kilometre (five mile) route that takes you through the inner west of Sydney, with an ever-present view of Iron Cove. I had an ulterior motive beyond enjoying a beautiful spring day and keeping fit: team think.

"Julie, we will do this run and by the end of it we will have a name for my keynote," I declared as we took off from Drummoyne.

FINDING THE MENTAL BARRIERS THAT STOP US DOING WELL just was not cutting it. Speaker bureaus and meeting planners were complaining to me that I needed to change it, so I took on their advice. I knew what I had researched and spoken about for the past three years was something that really resonated with a very broad range of audiences: truck drivers, lawyers, Year 11 students, boards of directors, and the majority of my audience – those involved in sales.

"It's obviously to do with the brain," I chirped as we hit an incline," *something to do with a barrier, a blockage...maybe Brain Buster?"* I received a crinkled nose face for this attempt. It sounded a bit macabre.

I had recently read a fantastic book by Sam Horn titled *POP!* – see the Recommended Reading section at the end of this book – so I knew the value of a brand that could stand out. From out of nowhere, Julie had it:

"What about Brain Blinkers?"

You know those moments. Maybe it was the first time you met your partner, or the moment you read the job description of your dreams in the newspaper – the moment you say THAT'S IT! When conditions in your life all of a sudden release the accumulated tension – like a rubber band, stretched and twisted for a long time – you get whacked on the head with bucket loads of relief, joy, clarity and excitement!

I could have kissed her, and I did! From that precise moment onwards, my topic/ keynote/workshop/book/passion would never be the same again.

When I hired a graphic designer to put together a logo that encompassed the brand essence of Brain Blinkers, I was expecting another one of those moments, and it happened when he came to me with the logo you see on the front cover of this book, although I did not kiss him.

Horse Blinkers

The horse racing industry uses blinkers, also known as blinders, to help keep the horse focussed on the path ahead. Blinkers help the horse remain calm by removing the distraction of the crowd or other horses and jockeys in the hustle and bustle of a race. For horses, blinkers are a good thing. These animals do not naturally race in this fashion, so human intervention has created a tool that can assist the horse and jockey in completing the task effectively and with minimal anxiety.

Similarly, Brain Blinkers are a human innovation. Effectively we place "blinkers" on our brain to shut out things we do not want to see. The blinkers are barriers that we consciously or unconsciously erect over the course of our life, according to our genes and our upbringing our "nature and nurture." Arguably, we erect these mental barriers in order to protect ourselves from our environment and from our enemies. Whatever the rationale, the most important thing to recognise is that Brain Blinkers exist, and that they can affect us in a very dramatic way.

How do we know we actually have Brain Blinkers? Read the following statements and see how you feel:

- The way I am is the way I am – I cannot change
- I cannot lose weight
- Mum/Dad always told me never to XYZ
- I cannot learn a new language
- This always happens to me

4

- Studying is for smart people
- Leaders are only ever born
- I have always been rubbish at sport
- I get so nervous when asked to present in front of a group, it makes me sick

Do any of these hit home for you? The fact is that we ALL have Brain Blinkers at some stage of our life, and many of us have many Brain Blinkers for all of our life! The trouble is whether we are actually aware that we have them. Quite often, our friends, family, or co-workers spot them first: *"Gee, isn't Karen taking the news of the company changes badly? Her attitude stinks. What's her problem?"* Because of our conditioning, we are often oblivious to the way in which we actually process information on a daily basis.

This book is about how we can enlighten ourselves. It is about being awake to the fact that we harbour beliefs and thoughts about ourselves and the world that can limit our opportunities and success, limit our happiness. If we address even just a few of these Brain Blinkers, then we open ourselves up to a new world of possibilities.

The Moment That Changes Everything

On July 31, 2005, at approximately 7.30 P.M., we were in the delivery suite preparation room for the third day in a row. The previous two days were false starts, but it looked like there would be no more false starts and my heart started to sink.

They were very early, but they were determined to join this world. Eighteen incredible members of the medical staff were in the emergency delivery room to ensure that the 27-week twins arrived as safely as possible. With my head feeling full of lead, I sat holding Julie's hand as we both cried. An emergency caesarean section was performed and little Isabella – *tiny* Isabella –was taken from Julie and placed on a respirator. They took a few more moments to "find" baby Milan, and did the same for him. There just seemed to be so many people in the one room to deliver our two little babies – neonatal intensive care nurses, doctors, specialists – all for our two little ones. It was over very quickly – we only got a short glimpse of our twins as they were whisked away into intricately cabled humidicribs, with machines keeping them alive.

Isabella was born weighing just 790grams, Milan just 815grams. That is just over one and one-half pounds each on the old scale. They were born more than three months early, and earned a poor prognosis from a mortality and morbidity perspective.

I was steered away from the room as the doctors attended to Julie and received some words not intended to shock or harm, rather to set realistic expectations of what lay ahead.

"Now, Mr Bonnici, try to get some sleep, and hopefully your children will be alive in the morning."

It did not dawn on me at the time. It was only in retrospect that I got underneath the words to understand that this particular nurse was trying to care for us. It may not have sounded like it, but she was. The first night spent lying awake in my makeshift hospital pull out bed was a night of unparalleled mental anguish and fear of a journey that would prove to be a turning point in my life.

The next morning, not knowing if our babies were still alive, I faced the most harrowing walk of my life: the journey from my bed down a long hall to the neonatal intensive care unit (NICU). I vaguely recall every step feeling as if I was on the moon, moving slowly but not seeming to make ground. My vision was blurred and my stomach knotted in the most severe case of stage fright you could imagine. Then I was in the NICU, and I could not speak.

"Mr. Bonnici, they are both still with us. They are on respirators and are doing as well as can be expected."

I felt as if we had won the lottery. It is amazing how much perspective on life you get in moments like this.

I can probably speak for every parent and share the difficulty in expressing the bond you have with your child. When your children are in such a dark place at the very beginning of their life, it too is something extremely difficult to explain. After we both cried continuously for a day or two after the twins were born, tears of fear for what the future holds, I recall a moment of clarity with Julie that I firmly believe made an impact on the outcome of this situation. It was a moment of awareness that acutely affected our thinking, our hoping, our behaviour, and our actions.

In that moment, we accepted that we have absolutely *no control* over anything in our lives, except how we *choose to react* to the situations we find ourselves in on a daily basis.

Our twins' lives were in the hands of the excellent staff at Westmead Hospital. We could not control so many of their circumstances, such as when they both got septicaemia shortly after they were born and nearly died. We could not control the fact that their chances of long-term problems with sight, hearing, learning, development and heart dysfunction were greater than 50%. What we *could* control was how we reacted. We chose to react by being there every day, writing in their little NICU journals and believing that we were doing the very best we could in such a horrible situation. I reckon it worked.

We started to smile a lot more. So did the staff, and so did the other parents visiting their children. We started smiling because the alternative – crying and feeling completely helpless – was not helping the situation. We brought cookies in for the staff, which they loved, and generally attempted to be as positive as we could at every opportunity around the twins, even with that thick plastic barrier between us. When we had the first opportunity to hold their tiny little bodies, we did it with gusto. In essence, we positively bonded with our kids and the environment our kids were in, and I firmly believe this helped them get through their struggle.

I hope I am not giving the impression that we were anything close to super human. At certain times, the burden would get to us and we lost a little control, a bit like a release valve on a hot water system. As time went on, we needed the release valve less and less, and we were happier for longer periods. The change in our beliefs certainly had an effect on our wellbeing and on those around us.

Today, you would have no idea what Bella and Milan went through in the first three months of their lives. They are physically, mentally and developmentally exactly where every four year old should be; in fact, better in a number of ways. The only physical reminders we have are the scores of tiny white dots on both of their hands, marking where painful cannulas were inserted almost daily. Our paediatrician, lung specialist and the NICU staff are flabbergasted at how well the twins have thrived since their tumultuous entry into the world. Now we are not religious people, nor are we particularly spiritually-oriented, and I know that many will put their incredible success story down to God or Allah or karma or even just plain good luck. Maybe so, but we do know that our "victim" behaviour changed very quickly after we started believing we could make a positive impact, and that in turn affects the behaviour, actions and outcomes of others, including the twins.

The Undeniable Cascade

The circles of psychology and psychiatry accept that our cognitions, our thoughts and beliefs, have a direct effect on our behaviour, and our behaviour can have an effect on how we feel. For example, if we believe that we must do everything perfectly, our behaviour might be one of procrastination and slowness – nothing will ever be right. Similarly, if our behaviour is one of distance and distrust of others, this behaviour may reinforce a belief that "people can't be trusted."

For the purposes of Brain Blinkers, we use a very simple three-step process to focus on how changing our cognition changes our behaviour and thus our outcomes.

Believe → Think → Behave

What you hold true about something (your belief) will affect how you think (process information) and thus how you behave (act).

People who are racist effectively believe another group of people are less important than they are. This belief may start in childhood, such as attitudes picked up from a racist father, and leads to conscious and unconscious thoughts that are racist. From these thoughts, racist behaviour arises. It is an undeniable cascade of cognition through to action.

Cognitive behavioural therapists argue that changes in beliefs must precede changes in behaviours. If you think about this for a moment, it makes perfect sense. The tricky bit is to *believe* that a belief needs to change.

You may have experienced or heard the frustration in a therapist, a friend, a parent who is trying to help someone, only to realise that "They can't be helped – they simply don't want to change." Unfortunately, this is correct. This book is useless to you if you understand how your behaviour needs to change but are not willing to make the necessary cognitive changes in terms of what you believe and how you think. Think of someone in your life who gives you the impression that they will never change. They have made a choice, and it will become **self-fulfilling prophec**y. A self-fulfilling prophecy is a prediction that directly or indirectly causes it to become true, by the very terms of the prophecy itself, due to the link between belief and behaviour. Although examples of such prophecies exist in literature as far back as ancient Greece and India, credit goes to a 20th-century sociologist, Robert Merton, for coining and formalizing the phrase.

So what specifically are Brain Blinkers? Based on what I have read in the psychological literature and my experience as a practitioner in NLP, I believe there are three main Brain Blinkers: limiting beliefs, negative thoughts and fear. A chapter is devoted to each of these Brain Blinkers in order to study them in more depth, and draw them out of your mind.

Why bother working on Brain Blinkers? We already have discussed this a little. Brain Blinkers can affect our:

- Mood – emotional state
- Behaviour – including performance, actions, and social interactions
- Longevity

Brain Blinkers can explain a lot about people such as why they might be angry, nervous, awkward, stressed, and fearful or overwhelmed. Brain Blinkers might be the reason you feel "stuck" treading water, just waiting for life to take you somewhere.

Brain Blinkers might be the reason you have missed promotions, or why you never quite stick to that New Year's resolution. Brain Blinkers can undermine the best intentions in the world.

I am going to ask you to do something. Go to page 93 of this book, and in the MY THINGS TO WORK ON form, write down some things that are troubling you RIGHT NOW. They might be exactly the same things I have mentioned above or maybe not. Either way, dedicate 60 seconds to jotting down some of these things. Why? Because your "things" might come from a Brain Blinker or two. We do not know for sure just yet, but we will work on it as we go along. I promise.

Chapter 2: Limiting Beliefs

"I can't STAND drivers who don't wave when I let them in..."

Sydney drivers suck.

I guess if you live in any other city in Australia or indeed, around the world, you could probably remove the word Sydney and insert your city's name in front of this sentence. It feels as though the older I get, the worse other drivers become. They seem more aggressive and less tolerant; more selfish and less forgiving; angrier and less courteous.

It seems as though most people interpret the road rules as simply a "guide" that is more often flaunted than followed until the police catch them doing something wrong.

Picture this: you are driving on a heavily congested major road. You see a slip road to your left – in Australia we drive on the left hand side of the road – and of course, that lane is attempting to merge into yours. We have all been there, done that.

Everyone seems to be doing it correctly, merging one car in front of the other, each taking a turn from the slip and then the major road to merge. The driver in front of you just let someone in from the slip road, and then it was the other driver's turn. It is your turn to let in someone. They do not use an indicator. They forcefully push in and do not even acknowledge your gesture with a little wave. In fact, they push into the next lane and force another car to brake suddenly, and you hear the obligatory horn blast from the wronged driver.

How do you feel? Does your blood pressure rise? Do you feel emotionally violated by this driver's rudeness, and was the phrase "You rude $#@%!" uttered? Do you yell something at him? Do you give him the one-finger salute? Worse still, do you start an argument – verbal or physical – with this guy?

You are experiencing road rage and they might be, too. Clearly, they are a bad driver, and they are the one who has done wrong, but who is the real idiot in this scenario? You may be a little upset by what I am about to put forward.

Road Rage is ridiculously common, and results in the death and injury of far too many people. Disgracefully, "road rage" is becoming a part of our society. A leading Australian motor vehicle insurer conducts a national survey each year to establish the key behavioural issues topping the AAMI Crash Index of 2009, based on a national survey of 2,500 licensed Australian drivers. Here are some of the disturbing findings as they relate to road rage:

- 91% of drivers say we are becoming more aggressive
- 60% worry about being a victim of road rage
- 29% have been followed after a road rage incident

The most concerning evidence is that our behaviour has changed as a result:

- 63% believe tailgating is a justifiable response to an act of aggression
- 83% say yelling, swearing and rudely gesturing are justifiable

Can these beliefs do damage? You bet, and it can happen to the best of us.

Car Wash Rage

One sunny Sunday morning in spring, I took my car to the local car wash. It is a "do-it-yourself" car wash – four large washing bays with a high-pressure hose in each, and you pay only for the time you use in the bay. The machine lets you choose the type of cleaning you want, from simple high-pressure water cleaning through foaming brushes and wax application. It is a modern man's delight, and something I actually enjoy doing.

As you probably know, a sunny Sunday morning in spring is the worst time in the world to visit a car wash, as every man and his dog is there, as it was this time: two cars were waiting for each wash bay except for the first lane, where no one was waiting. I proudly drove up behind the car in bay one. I tend to pick the longest queues in McDonalds, so I was happy with this choice.

To make the situation even better, the guy who was washing his car in bay one was on the final rinse cycle. I watched him finish rinsing his car, and put the high-pressure hose back in its holster on the side. So not only had I picked the shortest queue, I had the guy who was finishing first too! Woohoo!

Now all around this car wash are huge signs outlining what I thought was the most obvious, common sense message for the given situation: PLEASE DO NOT DRY OR CHAMOIS YOUR CAR IN THE WASH BAY. That is basic decency; you wash and rinse your car in the wash bay, then drive 15 metres to the drying bay where you can spend as long as you like vacuuming, drying, polishing and shining your newly cleaned car. Surely, they did not need to spend the money on these signs.

As soon as that rhetoric entered my head, the guy in my lane opened his car door to get something. You guessed it – a chamois. He started to slowly dry his car in the wash bay, and I now had two other cars behind me.

You are probably thinking, as I was, something along the lines of "how dare he?" How rude and inconsiderate is this man? Well, a similar thought ran through my mind as I stopped and thought about the situation. As I saw it at that moment, I had three choices: speak up politely, speak up not so politely, or say nothing. I immediately vetoed option three and with a few seconds of deep breathing also removed option two. I opened my car door and politely said the following, in a truly non-confronting and permissive manner:

"Excuse me mate, would you mind moving your car into the drying area over there so I can get in? Cheers."

He turned and puffed out his chest like a gorilla. I half expected him to beat his chest and drag his knuckles on the ground. As quick as a flash, he glared at me and yelled:

"Why don't you go back to your own f__ing country you black, f__ing wog."

For the next three seconds, I was in shock. He wanted me to go where? I was born here! He called me *what*? Is he serious? My mouth must have been gaping open. I know for a fact a few patiently waiting car washers wound down their windows to witness the fracas that was about to happen.

That was when the adrenaline hit me. I was absolutely propelled out of my car seat by something I had never felt before, a seemingly uncontrollable urge to do something to remedy the situation. I had no idea what I was going to do, but I was seeing red for the first time in my life and felt a strong urge to hit this guy.

Let me add some context here. I have never been in a fight in my entire life. I avoided fights at school by talking my way out of them. I was class captain from Year 5 through to Year 10. My school tie had so many badges pinned to it that it was actually heavy. As a quintessential goody two shoes and lifelong nerd burger, I probably would not know how to fight if my life depended on it, although at this particular point in time, this logic was not entering my mind.

Thank goodness, something else did actually enter my mind. As I started pacing towards this guy – he was half my size, but with his Michelin man chest costume pumped up to full, he looked bigger – my mind somehow interjected a visual into my consciousness. It was my eldest son William, then only six years old, and he was saying one simple thing:

"Dad, why are you at the police station?"

I froze in my tracks. I took a deep breath and walked back to my car, now with a smile on my face. I completely got it. Why on Earth would I put my safety in danger for the sake of this idiot? When it became logical, not emotional, it made me think of many other times in my life that I wish I could revisit based on this same principle.

In the end, this idiot moved his car out of the wash bay and into the drying area just five metres away. As I moved my car into the wash bay, got out of the car and grabbed hold of the high-pressure water gun, a fleeting moment of revenge surfaced in me like a cork on the tide. I could easily have doused him from where I stood. Common sense took hold, however, and I started to wash my car, and not his head.

The chirping of profanities was still in evidence from this red neck. He would shoot me a few death stares every minute or so as his mumbled list of four letter words made it over the sound of spraying water. Eventually, I thought enough was enough. I had taken the higher ground and chosen not to be upset about his incredible tirade of racist bullying. I now needed to finish it so I could continue washing my car in peace.

I calmly walked up to this guy, and he puffed up like the Michelin Man in one second flat. I looked him in the eye and said:

"Mate, it's Sunday and we are washing our cars. That'll do."

I smiled, but he did not. He just turned around, got back into his car, and without a sound, he just drove off. I walked away with a feeling of accomplishment, of success. Now Mr. Red Neck probably went home to his mates and bragged about he told off this wog at the car wash, how he gave me a piece of his mind and never backed down. Good luck to him: if that makes him feel like a man, then he has happy days coming. I have resolved to make choices not on what I have done to others but on how it makes **me** feel. It felt great to avoid a potential debacle and it still feels good to this day, actually.

If Only...

Road rage, or car wash rage, is not just frustration, anger, ill temper and impatience. It is not just reaction, primal instinct, fight or flight. Instead, the basis of road rage is the completely illogical belief that **everyone else should drive like us**. Everyone should indicate when they are turning, obey the speed limit, or wave when we let them in. Because that is what we do, right? I think this belief is completely asinine and nuts, so I will ask again, who is the **real** idiot?

Other drivers do not drive like us, and indeed will break the road rules. We have a very small chance of influencing their behaviour, let alone controlling how they drive, so why do we keep thinking we can? In fact, if we accept that we cannot control their behaviour, and that others will ALWAYS drive differently than us, then we can actually change something. We can choose to change our *own* behaviour, which, truly is the only thing in this world that we can control.

Try this on for size: the next time you are driving a car and face terrible traffic or crazy drivers – or both! – repeat this to yourself:

"I don't control them/this, nor do I wish to."

This is simple, but terribly effective. It will change how you feel and how you drive. Drivers who used to get up your nose no longer will do so. Traffic jams will be an inconvenience rather than the end of the world. You will start to feel less stressed and angry on the road, and your loved ones in the car with you will notice a difference.

I have to re-emphasise that I am not really into the world of self-affirmation and positive thinking. The ultra-loud music and the chanting at the motivational conferences really do not sit that well with me. I believe it has a place for some people, and good luck to them. I prefer to think of myself more as a pragmatist, a logical and yet passionate person who can see a good argument and reasoning when it is there. Moreover, I need to tell you that with my previously poor record in this area of road rage, this changed thinking made a massive difference to my family and me.

So Exactly What Is A Limiting Belief?

A limiting belief is a belief that holds us back from something. A limiting belief prevents us from moving forward, achieving a goal, making amends, or maybe from doing something we have always wanted to do. Limiting beliefs can strangle our performance and leave us feeling frustrated and angry, just as we do when we experience road rage.

Have you noticed what happens to our driving when we get angry on the road? We speed up. We drive more erratically. We "tailgate," or drive extremely closely behind other vehicles. We become more dangerous and susceptible to an accident. Unfortunately, the proof of this is the crash data mentioned earlier in this chapter.

Clearly, the belief that people should drive like me – they should indicate when turning, wave when I let them in, and stay out of the overtaking lane when not overtaking – is a **limiting** belief. All it does is increase my anger at other drivers, and thus negatively influences my performance – my ability to drive safely. The far more practical, logical, and safer belief to hold about other drivers is that they probably will not drive like me, and that is OK. This belief is infinitely more useful to us – it reduces the amount of damaging negative emotion we experience, such as anger and frustration, and allow us to be unconcerned about others as we drive our vehicle. Our driving improves, and we are less likely to injure or kill anyone on the road, which is exactly the outcome we need.

Do you remember the undeniable cascade from the previous chapter? What we believe dictates how we think and thus how we behave. The trouble is that we are often unaware of what we believe, or if we are aware of the belief, we do not recognise or accept the fact that the belief limits us.

A person with road rage may be aware that they are experiencing road rage, but remain unaware of **why** they are experiencing it – in this case, the belief that others should drive like them. They are therefore unaware that this belief limits their per-formance and happiness. When they become aware of this fact and take measures to alter the belief and thus the behaviour, life changes. I know this because it happened to me.

Einstein's Words

Albert Einstein did a lot for humanity. There is the understatement of the century! Although most know him only for $E=mc^2$, Albert Einstein's achieve-ments in the areas of science, mathematics, astron-omy, and philosophy are mind-boggling. Among his many famous interviews and quotes is a beautiful perspective on the topic of the mind and its trap-pings:

"We are boxed in by the boundary conditions of our thinking."

It took me three or four attempts to read this quote before I came close to understanding it. Einstein described the concept many years before behavioural psychology called it a limiting belief.

Just picture a million cages in your brain. There is a cage for everything you do. You have a cage for your ability to make money, one for how many friends you want in your life, another for your ability to sing, and so forth. Some of the cages are huge, and others are very small. Einstein put forward the idea that however large or small you make these cages, the boundaries around your beliefs and thinking, equates to your behaviour – what you do and how you do it. By deduction, to alter our behaviour and achieve more, we need to remove or reduce the boundary conditions. We need to bust open the cages.

Take this little test. Below are 10 statements. How many of these are true, or close to true, for you?

1. I am hopeless with names
2. I am rubbish at art

3. I do not have time to… (insert something you want or need to do, such as exercise)
4. Numbers are not my thing
5. I was born without a creative bone in my body
6. I just cannot hit… (insert a specific goal such as a sales target or financial goal)
7. I cannot lose weight because…. (insert excuse here)
8. I am too old to learn new things
9. I am not good enough or smart enough to study
10. I could never manage people

Did anyone get a perfect ten? Nine out of ten? Chances are, you scored at least three out of ten. That means you have three cages that are negatively affecting you. The cages boxing you in are too small, but nothing will change until you admit it. Admit that you have been telling yourself these things for a long time and they are the reason you have not done anything about it.

It is time to document your thoughts. Turn to "MY THINGS TO WORK ON" at the end of this book and write down the limiting beliefs that you now recognise. They might be in the list above or might be something else. This list is not exhaustive – there are hundreds of thousands of limiting beliefs floating out in the ether. Just a few minutes of your time to think and write – if you do this well you may need some more paper!

What's In a Name?

Take the first item in the list on the previous page: "I am hopeless with names." In my talks around the globe on Brain Blinkers, this one gets a big response. Now, think of what we are actually saying to ourselves. We are saying we cannot learn and remember people's names. We are going against the immutable law of learning and trying to convince ourselves that this one aspect of our ability to learn and memorise does not function. We may be able to remember other things, but names escape us.

You are about to meet someone, arm outstretched in preparation for the customary handshake. You look into the eyes of your new friend, thinking about what you are going to say next. They say their name, you say yours, and you launch into your quickly prepared small talk. Seconds later, you think to yourself *"what was their name?"* You have no idea. Did they even say their name? Maybe they did not. Panic sets in, as you now need to introduce this new person to someone else within the group.

You kick yourself in embarrassment. It always seems to happen to you; you almost immediately forget someone's name. It must be that you are simply terrible with names.

Does that ring a bell for anyone? Let us take a closer look at what is happening.

In the above example, we may intend to remember someone's name, but we do not have a *process* for remembering it. We are so busy trying to think about what we are going to say next – in order to appear intelligent, cute, witty, charming, etc. – we neglect to listen to the other person's name. This may be something we do a lot, or have done for a long time, or both. Either way, our conditioning to do it this way leads to the outcome of not remembering someone's name. Because we cannot see that there is actually an error in the way we are processing the interaction – we are too busy thinking about our next line instead of stopping to listen to the other person's name – we blame it on our inability to remember names. This process can go on for years, and in fact, many people go to their graves still believing they were hopeless at remembering people's names when it was simply an inability to listen at the right time!

I am not trying to say that we all have equal ability to remember names. That is ridiculous – some of us possess incredible memories and others with the ability to quickly process information, so there will always be a difference in individual ability to remember names. If you are telling yourself this right now, make sure you do not have the same or a similar blockage in the processing part of the equation. This mighty Brain Blinker – this limiting belief – might be the only thing that keeps you forgetting names constantly instead of remembering them.

Believing you are hopeless with names becomes a self-fulfilling prophecy. The more you say it, the more you tend to make errors in listening, and the more you forget names. It becomes a vicious cycle of self-doubt. The trick is to derail the autopilot somehow, to stop the automatic flow of events that occurs when we encounter a situation in which our conditioning causes us to do the same things. This next section will show us how limiting beliefs get a lot of grip because of this autopilot part of our brain.

Autopilot and 100 Billion Neurons

This book will not go heavily into neuropsychology and the anatomy of the brain or lecture on quantum physics and neuroanatomy. There is a little bit of neuroscience and neurobiology, however, that helps us understand how our Brain Blinkers take hold, usually from a very early age.

Long before we could understand what was going into our brain, most of what we hold true about life and the universe was implanted. Most NLP texts work around the magical age of seven because by that age, 95% of our beliefs are established in our brain. Think of our first twenty-one years of life as consisting of three phases: *imprint*, from birth through age seven (0-7); *modelling*, ages eight through fourteen (8-14); and *socialising*, ages fifteen through twenty-one (15-21).

The **imprint** phase is our earliest period, where we simply absorb information without any true cognition of what has gone in. Neurobiologically, the part of our brain responsible for decision making – the frontal lobes – are far from maturity, and so we do not actually have the mental capacity to make rational decisions during the imprint phase. Consequently, "whatever goes in just goes in." Parents, siblings, other family members, close friends and teachers are the main contributors of values and beliefs during the imprint phase.

Ages eight to fourteen see us **modelling** a specific parent or other adult, and ages fifteen to twenty-one see us moving away from family to engage in **socializing** with our social and tribal brain.

From this simplistic model, you can see that the first seven years of life are critical for the establishment of solid values and beliefs. These formative years explain much of the mental fabric of an individual, as every parent would attest. This is the time in a young person's life when we attempt to embed goodness, love, compassion, competitive spirit and individuality. During this time, a young person explores their world, pushes boundaries and tests their newly established theories of the world. We are naïve, energetic and willing to learn. In addition, we are laying down the foundations of a neural network that gives us astonishing abilities.

We all have approximately 100 billion neurons, or nerve cells, connected to each other to thank for our incredible potential to think and live. Each individual neuron can connect to 10,000 other neurons, making the potential number of connections possible in the human brain almost countless. Each connection, each neural pathway, represents a thought, a movement or an idea. These neural pathways keep us alive and breathing, regulate our temperature, and make sure there is enough moisture in our eyes. These neural pathways help us ride a bike, speak and love; they are nature's incredible mass of electrical wire.

Our brain forms new neural pathways all the time, and during the imprint phase, it works overtime. A new neural pathway forms when we learn something new. When a skill is reinforced and practised, it strengthens that neural pathway. Strong neural pathways become habitual, second nature. This autopilot feature ensures we do not have to be conscious of the hundreds of thousands of bodily functions regulated by our brain, or the millions of bits of environmental information from our senses processed by our brain.

Einstein estimated that if we were completely conscious of every single aspect of our being and the choices we need to make during just the first hour of waking, we would need to make 11,500 decisions. Einstein made this estimate sixty years before Facebook, Twitter and iPhones! Obviously, this is where our autopilot function is very handy – it leaves the decisions and functions of which we do not need to be constantly conscious to a specific part of the brain.

"SO WHAT?" I hear you say. Well, here is the rub: the fact that we have trillions of neural pathways, mostly hidden from our consciousness, is of particular consequence to us. It means that we all have the ability to harbour beliefs and thoughts engrained in us from an early age that they become second nature, habitual, and part of our autopilot. Now if these specific beliefs are helpful to us – such as "work hard to succeed" and "be good to other people" – then that is a good thing. We have them innately, and they come out in our personality and our daily interactions. Beliefs that are not so positive, or are limiting – such as "I am not good enough" or

"aggression gets results" – also can hide in our autopilot.

When these beliefs exist in our autopilot, we are not conscious of them. Therefore, if a limiting belief is in our autopilot unconscious system, then we can effectively live our life under the constraints of this belief *without ever being aware of it*. It may be frightening, but true, to realise that we can be boxed in by the boundary conditions of our thinking and our beliefs.

Ford vs. Holden

I grew up in a family that did not pay a lot of attention to motor vehicles. While growing up, unlike my cousins who really engaged with the classic Australian vehicular arm-wrestle of Ford vs. Holden – GMH for our American readers – I never really took sides in this Aussie debate, as I really could not care less.

As a young pharmaceutical sales representative, I received use of a company car, a Holden Commodore, so I had experience driving a Holden. I never had a Ford – my previous cars were a Toyota and a Honda –so I was not concerned with the discussion and debate between the two brands.

When the twins entered this world so prematurely in 2005, the car was one of the interesting decisions that had fallen by the wayside during the commotion of extreme prematurity. Julie and I had planned to buy a bigger vehicle to accommodate the two new additions safely, as well as our then two-year-old William. The Honda had only two harness anchor points for safety seats, so at some stage we had to find a vehicle with three, and was big enough to fit three car seats in the back seat and a double pram in the boot or trunk.

To cut a long story short, I had narrowed down the decision to one of two second-hand vehicles: a Holden Commodore wagon and a Ford Falcon wagon. In Australia at that time, both vehicles were very similar in looks, features, performance, safety and unit sales. The Ford had won Car of the Year in 2004, and to my very simple motoring eye, it was a little more aesthetically pleasing. It was also at least $1,000 cheaper than the Holden in the second hand market when you compared like with like, so things were starting to stack up significantly for the Ford. In fact, after utilising an Excel spread sheet to document the comparison – there is that nerd burger again – I realised it was a "no-brainer" decision.

Do you know the feeling when you face a no-brainer decision? It is easy, you feel comfortable, and you go right in and make the decision. Your homework is done and you are relieved that the decision is now beyond all reasonable doubt. Go forth and multiply.

Nevertheless, I could not make that decision if my life depended on it.

For some reason, I was procrastinating on making the decision. I kept asking my wife if she liked the headlights on the Ford or the Holden in a pathetic attempt to gain input. For weeks, I was in this state of flux, letting the tide of procrastination and ineptitude wash over me until I felt like I was drowning. Then one day, Julie just grabbed me and said "WHAT IS WRONG WITH YOU? JUST BUY A BLOODY CAR!"

Of course, she was right. I was going to write that she is always right but that would start a fight. I just had to decide. Before I could do that, however, I had to understand what was holding me back from making this seemingly no-brainer decision.

I thought for a few minutes. What is wrong in this equation? What is stopping me from doing this? What is it about this choice that bugs me?

Every time I ask these same questions in front of my audiences, I receive consistent responses: I was worried about bringing the kids home in *any* car; I was not happy with either brand; I had underlying concerns about the safety of both brands. Interestingly, none of these was true.

The real reason was that my father hates Ford.

Yes, he *hates* them. Why? Because in the early 1980s, Dad bought a Ford Econovan, one of the earliest "people-movers" promoted to families. He believed he was doing the best thing for his growing family of four children with another one yet to come, but Dad soon discovered that the vehicle was not as he hoped. He swore that he bought the model without brakes, and he disliked the drive. My memories are of a long red van that used to "bunny hop" a lot when the jump between gears causes the vehicle to "hop," but maybe that was due to his driving. My most clear recollection was of Dad cursing the car beneath his breath – always cognisant of kids in earshot – mumbling that the car was rubbish and why did he ever buy it.

Therefore, dad made his mind up about Ford from the experience of one solitary vehicle. That is fine, because we all do the same. We have one, or sometimes two or three experiences with something or someone, and then we make up our mind, we form an opinion, and we form a belief. Dad's belief was that Fords are rubbish, and he is completely within his rights to believe so. *Whether he is right or wrong has nothing to do with it* – he has a belief.

What happened was that I had an unconscious bias against Ford. I had no knowledge of or conscious preference for Holdens or Fords, but because of the unintended and unconscious influence of my father, I was 34 years of age when I was faced with a decision between vehicles – one that was obvious and clear in the given circumstance – and found my judgment clouded by an unconscious limiting belief. This belief, which did not really belong to me and had no relevance to me, was surreptitiously passed from my father during the imprint phase of my life, conditioned my thinking, and stuck with me for nearly thirty years.

I remember smiling like the Cheshire Cat when I realised this.

Can We Change Limiting Beliefs?

A long time ago, the answer would have been "NO." We accepted creationist theory that we are born with certain levels of intelligence, warmth, happiness, and so forth, and that was that. Work with what you have; do the best you can.

Plato spoke about the super powers of our words and thoughts, and although he effectively started a movement, acceptance came when Sigmund Freud put forward the law of association by simultaneity – the idea that our thoughts could change our brain wiring and thus our outcomes – that we came close to understanding the potential power of our brain. Apart from performing its basic physiological functions in *response* to our beliefs and thoughts, the brain could actually change and adapt *because* of our beliefs and thoughts.

This major development in the area of brain science, **neuroplasticity**, introduces the notion that our brain is much more malleable and changeable than we previously thought. Considered one of the biggest breakthroughs in brain science in millennia, it has implications in just about every facet of our lives, from education and training through space travel and medicine. The work of illustrious scientific researchers such as Eric Candell and Norman Doidge, the author of an amazing book titled <u>The Brain That Changes Itself</u>, is proving that our thoughts can turn on genes in our brain nerve cells that consequently connect with other nerve cells to produce new neural pathways. Our beliefs and thoughts can stimulate changes in brain physiology that we believed happened only during the early growth stages of life.

Let us go back to the question. From what we now know, and doubtless will continue to learn about the unquestionable power of our brain, we have the ability to change our thinking. We have the ability to change our beliefs, and in turn, to create changes in our brain that help us bring new possibilities to the journey of life. (More "how to" in Chapter 5.)

For the record, I bought the Ford Falcon wagon on the very same day I realised I had this limiting belief. My old man still thinks I was an idiot for doing so.

The Impact of Change

I wanted to share this small example because of the "3R" rule, which asks, "Is it real? Is it relevant? Is it recent?" For me, it is an example of how, regardless of your current age or what your conditioned beliefs may be, if you truly want to change your beliefs, you can.

I love performing. I have been a public speaker since I was young, and have had a passion for singing in bands for at least twenty years. Curiously, I hated music at school and thus did not study music during my higher education, but I jumped at the chance of forming a rock band with my mates in 1987. What a great way to pick up girls, I thought at the time.

I was a self-taught guitarist and vocalist, but eventually took singing lessons in the mid-90s to continue to improve my voice. Focussing on performing music I liked to listen to – The Beatles, Stones and lots of 70s and 80s pop music – I never took time to learn how to read music. I thought it was unnecessary; I had good ears for music and could pick out the chords to most songs. At the time, I did not realise the consequence of this belief.

Around 2005, I received an invitation to sing with a fantastic Big Band called the *Birdyard Big Band*, a band with which I continue to enjoy performing today. This 18-piece swing band was looking for a singer, so in my typically optimistic style I thought I would give it a go. It couldn't be that hard, could it?

I distinctly remember walking into the school library where the band rehearsed on a Monday night. My heart was beating fast as I politely said hello to the band members. They formed a large circle in the main room of the library, and to put it simply, I was intimidated. I did not realise this at the time – I just put it down to first timer's nerves – but a number of things were intimidating me. The size of the band, the impressive musicianship of each member, the quality of the sounds they were playing, and, most of all, my own self-doubt. Was I up to this? Was I about to overstep my capabilities? I could not read music, and these guys read music like reading books. Was I good enough?

I remember the sound of my voice as I cautiously and nervously started the first tune – the classic *I've Got You under My Skin*. I missed my introduction and was not sure about the key I was singing – basically, it was rubbish. I also remember looking around the "circle of intimidation" and trying to get a smile or some sort of acknowledgement that I was even close to being on track with the song, but got nothing back– I was on my own.

I knew it sounded ordinary, and being so conscious of this fact made me even more nervous. Consequently, the second song was no better, and the third was even worse. When we took a break, I was very close to leaving and not coming back.

During the break, the band's bass guitarist, the guy who suggested I audition, came up to me. *"Are you OK mate? You sound very nervous."* Steve had played in bands with me for over thirteen years. He knew what was going on.

"I think I'm out of my depth mate. They are all brilliant, and I can't read a note. I just feel wrong." My belief in self was shot and I honestly was ready to admit that I had bitten off more than I could chew.

"Did you listen to the songs?" Steve asked.

"Yes, of course" I replied. I wanted to make a good impression so I had learnt the tunes very well.

"Then just get up there and do them. You'll be fine; you can sing this stuff. Think of it as just another gig."

Steve is no master of psychology, but he said the exact right thing at exactly the right time. I just needed to back myself. I needed to get rid of the rubbish in my brain before I could perform. I was reinforcing the following limiting beliefs to myself:

- I am out of my depth
- I cannot read music, and therefore I am not worthy to be in this band
- Maybe I cannot sing Swing

The tea break gave me a chance to gather my thoughts and think about how I was mentally approaching this new challenge. I recall striding back into the room with a smile on my face, confident in who I was and what I was doing. I asked if we could go back to *Under My Skin*, and as the band started the riff at the beginning of the song, I remember smiling.

I was recalling the many times I performed very different songs to small and large audiences, and the looks on their faces, as a few of them would say to the people around them "I *love* this song!"

I started singing, and it worked. It was flowing nicely, my heart was in the performance and I felt like a changed man. The difference in the quality of the singing was amazing; so much improved that one of the saxophonists glanced over at me with a knowing smile. Boy, that made an impact. I continued the song – and the rest of the songs that night – with a completely different sound and feel.

I changed my behaviour and my performance by simply acknowledging and removing a limiting belief. That is a very handy skill to possess, don't you think? The best news is that you can learn to do this same thing quite easily.

Chapter 3: Self Sabotage

"We have enough people in this world telling us how rubbish we are, let alone saying it about ourselves."

Negative thoughts. Negative self-talk. Faulty thinking. Irrational beliefs.

In behavioural textbooks, they take on many names. For the intents and purpose of this book, we will call them techniques of self-sabotage. Put simply, they are faults and glitches in our own thinking systems that cause us to self-destruct, or at the very least sabotage ourselves in order to prevent pain. They are counterproductive, even though their purpose, to protect us, is noble.

The work of many behavioural psychologists in this area is notable. Albert Ellis and Aaron Beck – considered the fathers of behaviourism and the pioneers of Cognitive Behavioural Therapy (CBT) – outlined dozens of self-defeating thought patterns and behaviours. They found that many of us are predisposed to thinking this way, and we do it because we believe it may protect us from an unwanted outcome. In fact, self-sabotage does the opposite – it makes things worse and can lead to procrastination, addiction, abuse and neglect of self and of those close to us.

Self-sabotage can be a cultural phenomenon. For example, a typically Antipodean approach to life is the "tall poppy syndrome." That is, if one rises too far above the rest of us, we need to chop it down. We see this cultural attitude in our approach to celebrity whether it be politics, music, sport or any other industry that puts people on pedestals. While we may like our super heroes, we expect them to be like us when they are "off stage." We want our rock stars to be the best in the world on stage and when they return to reality, we need them to be down to earth. If we sense an attitude of arrogance or stuffiness, we want to bring them down to our level. Cut down the tall poppies.

We can see the implication of this in many aspects of our society. Kids on the sporting field may actually hold back to avoid appearing special and thus risking potential criticism from their mates. Workers are reluctant to sing their own praises – even if it means the difference between a promotion or not – because they want to be seen as equal with their colleagues.

Even the world of rock music is not immune. An interesting article in the Sydney Morning Herald in October 2010 spoke of how Australia had not produced a true "rock star" since Michael Hutchence of INXS back in the 1980s. Not for want of strong contenders: there is a long list of very successful artists, but no strutting, high-energy audacity like that of Hutchence, Jagger and Mercury.

Bernard Fanning – lead singer of one of Australia's premiere rock bands *Powderfinger* – summed it beautifully. When approached by the author of the article for comments on why he does not engage in the rock star approach to his performances, he replied with this:

"I've had that great Australian fear that my mates are going to give me shit."

Grab a COFFEE

Because I am a simple man and I like easy ways to remember things, I have chosen to outline the six most common ways in which we engage in self-sabotage. The following COFFEE acronym will help you remember the six key ways we press the self-destruct button.

I have structured the COFFEE section to mimic a medical consultation. Your doctor will look for **symptoms** in order to give you the diagnosis of a condition. He or she will also need to assess the **impact** of these symptoms on your ability to maintain a quality of life, and then they will **treat** you (we will get to the treatment part in Chapter 5). They may even share a **story** with you about another patient with a similar condition to ensure that you do not feel alone. For now be a good patient and focus on symptoms, impact and the story.

Note to self: As I go through the COFFEE model, I will actively flick to the MY THINGS TO WORK ON section and document the bits relevant to me. I will do this because it will help me get rid of my Brain Blinkers!

C is for CATASTROPHISING

Terrible word, I know. I made it up. Ellis used the term AWFULISING, which I think is just as bad, but I am sure you get the idea.

SYMPTOMS:

- Crying over spilt milk
- Making things out to be bigger than they really are
- Acting like a drama queen or king
- Feeling like the world is against you
- *Nothing* ever goes your way – lots of absolute statements, black and white thinking
- Big drama if something is not done *perfectly*

IMPACT:

- Anger and frustration
- High blood pressure, GI problems
- Stress and inability to cope
- Friends, family and co-workers ostracising you

A STORY:

The strength of conviction of our beliefs often leads to catastrophising behaviour.

I believe it is important to be on time for things. Whether it is a business appointment or meeting a friend for a drink, I always make sure I am on time or a little early. I have always done so, and always will, as I consciously believe that being on time is a mark of respect, and respect is a very important value to me. Therefore, you can see that anything that may get in the way of me being on time for something may be a problem.

It is not surprising that a personal source of catastrophising occurs when I misplace my car keys. Frantic searching increases my blood pressure and angst, causing me to speak loudly and accusingly at others in the vicinity – usually my wife – and thus inflame the situation. Inevitably, someone with a cooler head finds the keys – my wife, again – and then I would slowly return to the normal me.

Does the strength of the underlying belief validate the act of catastrophising? I believe not. The underlying belief, such as respecting people's time, may explain the act of catastrophising, but it does not validate it. We need to be responsible for our own actions, so if the act of catastrophising brings harm to us or to the people around us, then the behaviour needs modification. I need to be more careful where I place my keys. Simple as that – I need to make changes that can reduce my catastrophising and maintain my value of being on time.

Has it worked? Absolutely, but I am certainly not perfect. I still misplace my keys, but because of the processes I have implemented to change my behaviour, it happens much less often and with much less intensity.

O is for OVERGENERALISING

Overgeneralising is the art of putting people and things into a box, a pigeonhole. Matching like with like may be necessary for our survival and our decision-making, but when done too often it can lead to mistakes and poor judgement. Racism is a classic overgeneralisation, in the sense that we put all the people of one culture or background into one basket. The same applies to religions, and we are all too well aware of the problems that exist in that realm.

SYMPTOMS:

- Quick to judge others
- Dismissive of others
- Close mindedness
- Arrogance

IMPACT:

- Small, myopic group of friends and acquaintances
- Deep seated anger and dislike for certain pigeon-holed groups

A STORY:

It was the first day of my bachelor's degree in business, University of Technology, Sydney, January 1989.

I was nervous, excited and keen to make a good impact on my first day. No other friends from school chose this degree, so I was there on my own. This took place before the Web era – many readers are now shaking their heads in disbelief – on the day we enrolled into the appropriate classes for our major. The smart kids planned their morning well and lined up early for the best classes – tutorials and lectures – to minimise the amount of days they needed to be at university. As it worked out, I was one of those planning to minimise time spent at university, as the trip in from my family home in the suburbs was a good 45 minutes each way.

Before too long, I had successfully put my name down for all but one of my subjects, and was well on my way to scoring a Tuesday/Wednesday/Thursday program, such that all of my subjects were crammed into just three days at university – a fantastic result. I just needed to lock in this one last tutorial. The queue was about eight people deep, and it was going to be touch and go.

So there I was, nervously tapping my foot as I waited in line. I was so excited about scoring such an excellent university program that I had neglected to notice the stunningly beautiful woman standing in front of me. When I finally did, I was gobsmacked. She had long blonde hair, a perfect figure, and delectable posture, and I was a single young man of 17 and a half.

In 1989, I was quite a shy guy, especially around girls. Low in self-confidence, I never really had the courage to walk up to a girl and start talking. I stood there, hands clasped and eyes up in the air, wondering if there was any hope that she would turn around and say hi. Just a brief turn and smile would do.

Then it happened.

Blonde locks flailing, she turned and said, *"Hi, I'm Amanda."* I swear her teeth did that sparkly thing you see in cheesy movies and in toothpaste commercials.

"Hi, I'm Anthony," I replied with an obvious tone of *I cannot believe she is talking to me*.

"What's your major?" she asked, with a smile that would kill a small dog.

"Finance and Economics" I blurted. There is no way this beauty would be doing finance, I thought, probably marketing or communications.

"Me too!" she yelled, much more excitedly than I would have picked, which gave me enormous encouragement. Could she possibly be the most beautiful nerd burger in the world?

"What days are you doing the tutorials?" I pried, in hopeful anticipation that she may actually be in one of my classes.

"I'm aiming for a Tuesday, Wednesday Thursday program. I just need this subject to make it all happen."

I froze. She was going to be in ALL of my classes. On only the first day of university, all the luck going my way. How good is life?

"Have you got far to come in to uni?" By now, I was calming down, starting to think and act a little more smoothly. Surely, the Gods were looking down on me now.

"No, not at all. How about you? Where do you live?" Hers was a much more pointed question than mine.

I was in a dilemma. You see, I grew up in the western suburbs of Sydney. For those who do not know the geographical, socioeconomic and cultural finesses of Sydney, the suburb in which I was born and raised was very working class. Unfortunately, the media often incorrectly portrays Blacktown as a suburb fraught with the evils of drugs, alcoholism and violence. Yet my four younger sisters and I grew up to respect the people around us, to be good to others and work hard at what you do to go places in life.

The dilemma was to tell the truth or lie and tell her that I came from a more affluent suburb, in order to appear more socially acceptable.

My mother taught me never to lie. I said *"Blacktown."*

Her face told the story. Her eyebrows raised, her eyes sort of glazed over. She literally took a step back and said, *"Oh."*

That was nothing. What she did next was the best.

She turned away from me and literally walked away from the queue we were in and joined the end of another queue.

I am serious. This is a TRUE STORY. If it had not happened to me, I would not believe it either. This woman just upped and walked away as soon as she heard the B word: Blacktown.

I stood there with my jaw open, not comprehending what just happened. Did I accidentally spit in her face? Does my breath reek? Did I forget to shower? All the questions I asked myself as I stood there in line with Snow White vanished. It slowly dawned on me that she engaged in a wonderful example of overgeneralisation, although I did not quite know that terminology back then – I just thought she was snobby.

She heard the "B word" and immediately put me into a pigeonhole, whatever that meant to her, and her overgeneralisation meant **she** was missing out – at least that was what I told myself.

F is for FILTER

When we want to, we can be very good at tailoring what we hear. Negative filtering occurs when we choose to hear only the negatives in a given conversation, despite the presence of multiple positives. It is selective hearing, usually performed by people with high expectations of themselves and commonly regarded as perfectionists. If you are tough on yourself, make sure you pay particular attention to this one!

SYMPTOMS:

- Very keen for feedback in order to "improve themselves"
- Seems to remember only negative or constructive feedback from any interaction
- Continues to focus on negative feedback for hours, days, and weeks after the initial conversation
- Gets upset with a result of 18 out of 20 on an exam or project and obsesses over where those two points went

IMPACT:

- High level of constant stress, GI upsets
- Mood fluctuates severely, bouts of depressive episodes
- Others reluctant to give any more constructive criticism or feedback as they fear the person will react badly or focus on it inappropriately

- May lead to "cotton-wooling" – they are protected from the truth

A STORY:

Mary is 16 and working her first part time job at a hamburger restaurant. When she has been there six weeks, her boss calls her into the office.

"Mary, I just wanted to give you some feedback now that your probation period is over. Look at this graph. It shows how our sales have had a sharp increase. It corresponds to the time you started here. It is such a big jump that I did a bit more homework to find out more."

"What I found was that since you have been there, our customer satisfaction survey result have turned on their head. We used to receive only complaints, now it seems we are only getting positive comments about our service and our products."

"Your energy, enthusiasm and positive attitude make a massive impact on the people you work with, and therefore our customers and our results. You are always on time; you show respect to everyone here, and you are keen to do a great job. You are so keen in fact, that sometimes your shirt gets untucked at the back, but who cares. You are a superstar, and I never thought I would say this, but you are most certainly in line to become a manager at the tender age of 16! We love having you here, keep up the excellent work, and here is a nice little bonus as my way of saying thanks."

Wow!

Mary, however, walks away from the conversation with a slightly concerned look on her face, thinking, *"My boss thinks I'm untidy."*

Are you like Mary? Do you choose to remember only the negatives? Maybe this is how your thinking is ingrained – remember the autopilot function – either way it needs to change. Filtering is a very common technique of self-sabotage and is one of the most dangerous because it can lead to lots of self-esteem problems and in its worst form, can lead to serious mental health issues.

The tool we will share in Chapter 5 will really help you if you consider yourself a filterer.

F is for FORECASTING

Have you ever met someone who just loves to pooh-pooh an idea based on their immense experience? They usually puff their chest out, cross their arms in front of them and bellow, *"That will never work here."* These people are negative forecasters. They are predicting the future, just without a head-scarf and crystal ball. They predict it negatively and therefore pre-empt the result – everyone likes to be proved right, right?

SYMPTOMS:

- Quick to summarise situations/projects and quick to add in their negative evaluation
- Say 'no' much more than they say 'yes'
- Constantly refer to their years of experience
- Like to share their negative views with others in order to ensure that their point of view is achieved

- Say things like "I tried it before, it didn't work then, so it won't work now"

IMPACT:
- Friends and colleagues do not seek their input
- Engaging in work/social conflicts
- Virtually no positive input into creative thinking or problem solving

A STORY:

For the six years I was in senior sales and marketing management, I could almost predict every year whether we would achieve our brand sales target based on the presentation of the target to the sales force in the first month of the sales cycle, typically in January for a calendar year of sales. I did this by simply watching the reaction of the audience to the announcement of the target. I was looking for how much negative forecasting would exist.

We always started by showing the sales force how we came up with the sales target: market and brand trends, competitor analysis, promotional strategy, product messages, supporting materials and cycle plans. This was something every sales organisation did with their teams at the beginning of the sales cycle. We would then unveil the target, as the team now had a good understanding of how we got there. Every year was a stretch target, and explained as such.

I observed one of two general reactions of the group over the many years. If the group nodded their heads and gave generally positive body language cues when announcing the number, chances were good that we would hit the target. We did this for a number of brands where we received that response over the six years. On the other hand, if we received the opposite response –surprised faces, shaking of heads, arms folded, and a generally negative response, our chances were gone. It would not matter how logical or achievable the target actually was. Facts had nothing to do with it: negative forecasting is an emotional dynamic.

During the break in proceedings, everyone would be speaking about the target. People engaging in negative forecasting would be telling everyone else why the target is unachievable, due to their previous experience selling that product. What they were generating was self-fulfilling prophecy, not only for themselves but for the people they had now infected their negativity with. Logically they still wanted to achieve the target and get bonuses and a sense of achievement, but they had disarmed this ability by forecasting negatively.

E is for EMOTIONALISING

As humans, we revel in emotion. It is at our core and involves everything we do. Emotions can define us, but like everything in life, there needs to be balance. If we take things too personally, we run the risk of becoming an emotional wreck. Emotionalising is when we fail to separate *who we are* from *what we do*, especially as it relates to negative emotions. For example, when we make a mistake in life or fail at something, then that is what we have done. People who emotionalise take this to heart and believe that they are a failure because of it: *I have failed at this specific thing; therefore, I am a failure.* That is not the case – you are choosing to believe that.

SYMPTOMS:

- Low or depressed mood
- Unwillingness to commit to doing anything substantial or major
- Fear of failure
- Demotivation, poor attitude

IMPACT:

- Depression and other mental health issues
- Procrastination
- Lack of commitment
- Low or poor productivity

A STORY:

Second year at university was critical for me. I learnt a very valuable lesson from a severe case of emotionalising.

As someone who is very hard on himself and is always trying to be the best at everything (see our previous self-sabotage technique of filtering), I prided myself on a very strong academic record during school. In fact, I cannot recall failing a single thing in my life until I met my match with Managerial Cost Accounting.

From the outset, I hated the subject. I loathed the lecturer, who was also our tutorial leader, and the subject simply did not click for me. This made me even more frustrated, as I had never encountered a subject that I could not get my head around. As the semester dragged on with angst, frustration and determination, and culminated in the final exam. I was giving it my all, but felt unusually perturbed as I left the examination room. I thought I would just scrape through.

I got 48%. I had no idea why I did not receive a conceded pass, but I failed the subject.

I learnt about my fate whilst on summer holidays with friends. The report card read something like this:

Subject 1:	HD
Subject 2:	D
Subject 3:	C
Subject 4:	D
MCA:	Z

A failure at UTS Sydney was a **Z**. How final is that?! Not an F, but a Z. I remember reading it thinking there was obviously some mistake. It was not possible for me to fail a subject. No way. Unfortunately, it was true, and I would have to repeat the subject the next semester.

Rightly or wrongly, I was unbelievably ashamed. How could I fail? What a loser! These thoughts pervaded my conscious mind and I could feel my mood slipping downhill. In fact, if I look back at those months following the exam results, I was depressed and not much fun to be around – I do not know how my poor parents and sisters put up with me – all because I **chose** to equate failing in an exam with failing as a person.

Only after my mother encouraged me to wake up to myself and truly see how I was choosing to cope with the situation that I made changes. I shook off the emotionalising behaviour and belief, got back on track, and I passed the subject the next semester.

E is for EFFECTUALISING

Yet another terrible word, but I make no apologies. The final letter in the COFFEE acronym relates to the fantastic work of Roger Connors and Tom Smith with their landmark book on accountability, <u>The Oz Principle</u>. The book has spawned a huge leadership business (see more at <u>www.ozprinciple.com</u>), but importantly the heart and soul of the principle remains true. That is, in life we have the choice to be either **above or below the line**. When we are below the line, we are at the **effect** of others. We engage in behaviour that blames others, makes excuses, points fingers and walks away from accountability. We lack control of a situation and we are the victim. This paralyses our solution thinking, which is not a good place to stay. Road rage is the perfect example of being below the line, being at the effect of another.

Being above the line puts us at **cause**. Here – with the same set of issues, problems or challenges – we choose to ask ourselves "how can I fix the situation." It means putting your hand up, taking control, looking for a solution, being accountable. It may mean taking a higher ground, or looking more broadly for answers. Either way the important thing to realise is that you have infinitely more chance of finding a solution or getting a good result when you are at cause (above the line) rather than at effect (below the line).

Control

Solutions **CAUSE** Accountability

"How can I fix it?"

Blame

Victim Mentality **EFFECT** Complaining

No Control

SYMPTOMS:
- Blaming
- Finger pointing
- Complaining
- Victim mentality
- "It is not my area, problem or concern"
- Constant anger with the behaviours of others

IMPACT:
- Blood pressure and stress
- Avoidance of responsibility and results, therefore lower productivity
- Reduction or dissolution of social and business networks due to people not wanting to be around you

A STORY:

In my role as a speaker, I rely on many people to help make my "product" a powerful and successful one. I rely on the sound guy to ensure the microphone is fitted correctly and that my voice sounds good through the PA system. I rely on the client to have organised an agenda that allows enough time for me to do what I do. Before all of this even happens, I sometimes rely on speaker bureaus to represent me to potential clients in order for me to get the opportunity to speak in the first place.

When I feel that a bureau has not provided many opportunities for me to speak, I have two ways to react. One is to be below the line and accuse them of not supporting me, blame them for ineptitude and favouritism of other speakers, complain wildly that poor old Anthony never gets the appropriate opportunities. Surely their job is to represent me, so why are they failing to do it? Cue violins please.

I could choose to react by saying "what can I do about this?" This reaction would evolve into a small think tank. What are the potential solutions? How is my bureau communication plan? What have I done for bureaus in the past three months? Why should they know I even exist? What value do they seek from me? How can I really help them?

It took about 28 seconds to come up with those six questions. If I were serious about getting more work through bureaus, answering these questions and implementing the action plan would most certainly reap results. I am accountable, I am responsible and I will have a solution. Notice the number of times "I" occurs.

Where do you spend most of your time, above or below the line?

A Final Word or Two On Self-Sabotage

1. Now that you are aware of the six different ways you can commit self-sabotage, it is important for the following to remain top of mind:

    - Remember that many of the symptoms and impact of self-sabotage relate to one's mental health. If you feel depressed or have any mental health concerns whatsoever, it is vital that you contact the relevant medical authorities in your country, whether it is your local doctor, hospital or mental health professional.

2. Become more self-aware and notice when you are self-sabotaging

    - Get others to help you do this – people love to help! Appoint someone at work or home to catch you when you are forecasting negatively, or when you are catastrophising. Remember most self-sabotage is hiding in autopilot!

3. Be careful not to confuse the behaviour with the person. The behaviour is the act of self-sabotage, such as filtering. Avoid labelling a person as a "filterer" – they are someone who may filter, but to label them is to overgeneralise!

So there you have it. Beware of drinking too much COFFEE!

Chapter 4: Fear

"I felt like a 12 year old girl at a Justin Bieber concert."

It had been a very warm morning, and a gorgeous Melbourne summer afternoon ensued. It was December of 2001, and I had flown down on a very early flight from Sydney for work. I went from the airport into meetings all day, and had some very productive discussions with some important people, so by the time 5.30pm came around, I was very pleased with how the day had progressed.

I was in a great mood: a strong sense of achievement and a fiery anticipation of the rest of the day. I planned to catch up with a friend I had not seen in many years, so I was naturally excited about the prospect of a chinwag and a few drinks with this person.

I got back to my hotel room, had a shower and got dressed. I took the lift down to the lobby and strode out as if I owned the place. I wasn't expecting anything to happen – I was just planning to catch a cab to our designated drinking hole.

Then he walked past me; no, *sauntered* past me. He had an air of power and presence, but was incognito with his dark sunglasses and bowed head. The long green and yellow luggage bag was a dead giveaway, and it didn't take me long to figure out who it was.

Wasim Akram was in the lobby of the Hilton.
Now, I apologise to those of you who are reading this and wondering about the identity of Wasim

Akram. If you don't know the masterful game of cricket, you surely won't know Wasim Akram.

Wasim is one of the legends of the game, and my idol. He played for Pakistan in the 1980s and 90s, and took 414 test match scalps. I just loved his bowling and batting skills when I was a youngster, and always pretended to be him playing backyard cricket in the summer months. He was walking in front of me in the Melbourne Hilton, so it was an opportunity that I was not going to miss.

I have been involved in public speaking for many years. I first started public speaking when I was 11, and took intensive coaching during after school hours until I was 14. Since then I have been involved in debating, public speaking eisteddfods, and many other speaking competitions, so I had lost the fear of speaking well before my adulthood. Friends and family would attest that I have never been short of a word, and never in my life have I been left wanting in a conversation.

In my confident state, I changed trajectory from the Hilton front door to reception where a guarded Wasim Akram was beginning to check in. I felt a surge of adrenalin as I approached, and as I got close to my idol, I saw him adjust. He realised that someone was approaching fast, so he removed his glasses and turned to face me.

I stretched out my arm to shake hands, and I remember looking up at an angle to greet him eye to eye – he is six feet two inches whilst I struggle to make five feet nine inches. His massive hand was there to greet mine as I confidently remarked:

"Hi Wasim, I'm Anthony and it is an absolute pleasure to meet you."

It was a warm and firm handshake, just what I had expected. He maintained solid eye contact with me and with a smile replied:

"It's a pleasure to meet you too, Anthony."

What a guy: a warm, friendly legend of cricket.

Then something happened. I didn't know why, but a force gripped me from that exact moment onwards. As I stood there still shaking his enormous and calloused hand, I knew it was my time to speak again, and I did.

"Ehh , balahhh aahh blaah aghh balah blejk"

I tell no lie; this would have been the literal translation of my complete and utter gobbledegook. I had become mind numbingly illiterate and it just flowed from my mouth like verbal diarrhoea.

Wasim the Great was left with no option but to react, in some way, and he did with the most subtle raising of his eyebrows, as if to say "what on Earth is going on here?" He must have thought that things were promising at first – a well-dressed, relatively eloquent and confident young cricket lover angling for some time with one of the game's greats – but it had fallen apart at the seams.

My mind was screaming "WHAT ARE YOU DOING?? SAY SOMETHING INTELLIGENT!" Isn't it amazing how your brain can engage but your mouth not?

So there we were, handshake finally over, cricket legend with an awkward look of embarrass-ment and empathy etched on his face, and an average Joe Blow cricket fan with a mouthful of marbles. Something had to give; I simply had to say something like "Wow, don't know what got over me, so sorry about that!" Something infinitely more funny and ridiculous surfaced.

"Ok, bye."

With that, I departed. If humans had tails, mine would have been firmly wedged between my legs. As it was, I felt like I was crouching – I probably was – and that my body was 10cm from the ground. I was actively looking for a hole in the ground of the hotel foyer, but couldn't find one. I made it through the door after what felt like four-and-a-half hours, and immediately burst into hysterical laughing. I recall laughing so much that it hurt my stomach, and to the passing Melbourne-ites, I must have looked like a certified lunatic.

So What Happened?

Fear: an unadulterated, certifiable and quite typical fear reaction.

Fear is one of our core and primal emotions, and – together with our massive brain – is one of the key reasons the human species still thrives today. Our physical size and lack of strength compared to most animals puts our species at a distinct disadvantage, so it is our ability to think, reason and react that puts us ahead of the pack. We will spend some time on this last aspect – how we react – in order to shed some light on the notion of fear.

What Exactly Is Fear?

Fear is an emotional response to a perceived threat. It arises in response to a stimulus such as the threat of imminent danger, and joins emotions such as sadness, joy and anger as our basic and innate feelings. It is a hardwired response designed to protect the species.

Charles Darwin, in his book <u>The Expression of the Emotions in Man and Animals</u>, described fear this way:

"Fear is often preceded by astonishment, and is so far akin to it, that both lead to the senses of sight and hearing being instantly aroused. In both cases the eyes and mouth are widely opened, and the eyebrows raised. The frightened man at first stands like a statue motionless and breathless, or crouches down as if instinctively to escape observation. The heart beats quickly and violently, so that it palpitates or knocks against the ribs. That the skin is much affected under the sense of great fear, we see in the marvellous manner in which perspiration immediately exudes from it. The hairs also on the skin stand erect and the superficial muscles shiver. In connection with the disturbed action of the heart, the breathing is hurried. The salivary glands act imperfectly; the mouth becomes dry, and is often opened and shut."

He was obviously describing me in the Hilton hotel.

The Nuts And Bolts of Fear

We have this physiological reaction because our parasympathetic nervous system compels the so-called "fight or flight" response, and causes the body to redirect blood flow away from the torso and head and towards the arms and legs so that one can fight their enemy or run away very quickly. This explains the many things that happen in our body when we experience fear, including:

- Heart rate increase, to get blood to arms and legs quickly
- Increased blood pressure, also to move blood into the extremities
- Muscle tightening, to prepare for fighting or running
- Increased perspiration, when the body senses more heat from blood flow, we perspire to cool down
- "Butterflies" in stomach, from blood leaving the gut
- Tunnel vision from the brain becoming single-minded in purpose
- Pupil dilation, because the eyes need more light to heighten awareness of surroundings

A specific and ancient part of our brain called the amygdala is responsible for fear, and is also largely responsible for our memory and emotional responses. When it senses danger, the amygdala sends a message to the adrenal glands, bizarrely located on our kidneys, to secrete a hormone called adrenaline into our blood. Adrenaline quickly initiates the fight or flight response, and we get that amazing adrenal feeling. Think of a time when you have been completely shocked or surprised by something – maybe you narrowly escaped a car accident or were terrified as you stood in front of 400 people for a presentation. That heavy feeling in your veins is adrenaline, preparing you to fight or flight!

Fear and Performance

You might have heard many conflicting perspectives about how fear can affect our performance. Some say it helps, others say it hinders, and some say it has no effect.

My seven year old shared his theory with me very recently. Before a tee-ball game, he exclaimed that he had butterflies in his stomach because he was a little nervous. Before I could say anything, he had reasoned he was happy with that, because it would help him hit the ball further. When I asked him where he heard that, he said that his teammate had told him. I wonder if William's teammate has heard of the Yerkes-Dodson Law.

This law describes the relationship between *arousal and performance*. Arousal in this case means the psychological state of awareness and activity in reaction to stimuli. Essentially, the more aroused we become, the better we perform, but only up to a point. After that point, the negative aspects of increased arousal on our ability to process information hinder our performance and can reduce performance outcomes.

Studies testing of the Yerkes-Dodson effect have confirmed the relationship between arousal and performance, and it also passes the gut feel test. We know that when we have some adrenaline flowing through our veins, we are sharper, more alert, more focussed and usually performing at a higher rate.

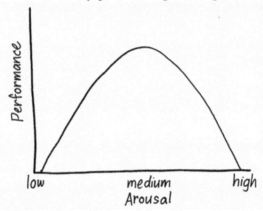

Some people call this "being in flow," and this is what happens on days when you come home from work or school and realise things have just fallen together and the day has flown by. You have hit that perfect level of arousal to keep you performing at your very best – at the top of the curve.

If we now substitute fear for arousal, we get a similar response. Use the following table as a gauge for comparing levels of fear and arousal:

	Low Arousal	**Medium Arousal**	**High Arousal**
Fear	• Not nervous • Normal attention • Normal breathing • Normal heart rate	• Some butterflies • Very focussed • Slightly tense, prepared • Breathing and heart rate higher • Feel "in flow"	• Very nervous • Jumpy, jittery • Unable to focus • Muscle jerks, shaking • Racing heart and breathing

With the above in mind, I like to think of the relationship between fear and performance as an inverse or upside down J curve, as shown below:

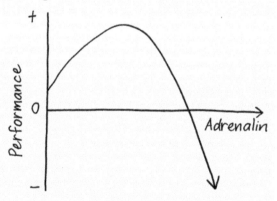

You can see that it is very similar to the Yerkes Dodson Law, although the result of extremely high levels of fear (adrenalin and arousal) is *negative*

performance. That is, we can actually perform much worse than we would with no arousal or adrenalin.

As you can see, low- to mid-level fear generates an arousal that I have termed energy, and it is at this level of adrenaline that the body derives more positives than negatives. Our heart rate and breathing rate increase to levels that make us feel strong and alive; we feel our blood pumping through our veins. Our mental alertness is at a level where we actually have increased peripheral vision, we can think methodically and logically "on our feet" and are confident of our ability to respond. Our muscles feel tighter but not cramped, and we seem to stand taller. We are alive and filled with **energy**.

This state helps us create our best work and our highest level of performance. Think back to the most recent time you felt like this. Maybe it was on the sports field, or maybe it was just prior to an exam. Perhaps you had just delivered your best presentation yet. The feeling is unmistakeable, and we feel bulletproof as a result. Use this as your new benchmark of the exact amount of fear, arousal and adrenaline you need in your system to perform at your best. For William, it is approximately four or five butterflies pattering around in his stomach, because he hit the ball like an absolute champion that day!

The trouble starts on the right hand side of the peak in this graph. Too much fear leads to a state of **anxiety**: heart rate and breathing seem excessively fast, nearly out of control and we become subject to hyperventilation. We start to shake, our legs quiver, our stomach turns, our head feels wishy washy and that sharp focus from just a moment earlier disappears. Our vision changes from extremely wide to very narrow, like a tunnel, and we start to have a lot of self-doubt. Have I remembered everything? Can I do this? What do I think I am doing here? The vicious cycle has begun.

Within seconds, our performance can plummet below the horizontal line like I experienced with Wasim Akram, or like you may have when you stuttered on stage and completely forgot your speech. I witnessed someone actually wet their pants on stage due to an immense and sudden fear impact. I have also witnessed catatonia, where one completely freezes and is motionless. In its worst cases, fear can really stop people in their tracks.

It doesn't have to get to that level, however, to really impact your performance.

Schipper's Zipper

Jessicah Schipper is one of Australia's living legends in the sport of swimming. She is an inspirational butterfly and 4 x100metre relay swimmer, with two Olympic and five World Championship gold medals to her name. Considered one of the darlings of Australian sport, she is a terrific competitor. Nevertheless, what happened to her performance in the 100-metre butterfly event at the 2008 Beijing Olympics was nothing short of astounding: Schipper proved the inverse J curve model beyond all doubt when she had a wardrobe malfunction that most likely cost her the gold medal.

The smart money was on Jessicah to win the gold medal in this, her pet event. Then, in the minutes before the marshals came to collect the swimmers for the final, the zipper on Schipper's swimsuit became stuck. Read this excerpt from the Sydney Morning Herald report on the incident from 2008:

The Queensland swimmer was in a panic in the immediate build-up to the final when her LZR Racer would not close properly, forcing her to frantically search for another suit.

When she emerged before the media after claiming bronze in a time of 57:25, tears were welling in her eyes.

"I had a bit of a hard time in marshalling," she said. "The suit wouldn't zip up. I had to get changed into an old suit. I'm just running on a bit of stress and adrenaline at the moment. It's all catching up with me."

A hard time in the marshalling? A bit of stress and adrenaline? I bet!

Obviously, poor Jessicah's adrenaline levels had shot up through the right hand side of the horizontal axis. It had an undeniable effect on her performance, and all she could do was be disappointed. Think about it – after training for so many years, swimming countless laps of a lonely pool nearly every day of your life in order to get to this moment, and then the emotion of a stuck zipper gets in your way. It's heartbreaking.

Modulating Adrenaline and Managing Fear

Interestingly enough, the corollary to Jessicah's story – a way in which you can positively manage your levels of adrenaline and fear – was demonstrated by another Australian Olympic swimmer during the same Olympic games, and amazingly, *during the very same final.*

Libby Trickett is another Aussie swimming superstar. Like Schipper she was an icon of the Australian swimming team, and someone we all love to love. She was in the final with Jessicah for the 100-metre butterfly, and had qualified fastest, just 0.03 of a second ahead of Christine Magnuson from the US, and 0.38 of a second in front of Schipper.

"I was really nervous before the race — I was almost sick in the marshalling area. But as I walked out for the race, I just thought to myself 'you have done the work, you have the confidence, now just do the job.'

"A nice feeling of calm came over me and I just thought that whatever happens, happens."

It happened alright. She got gold.

Isn't it a fabulous example of how we can actually control the amount of arousal/fear/adrenalin that we are faced with? She was basically dry reaching before the marshal entered to take them to the blocks. Imagine for a second how much physical and emotional energy is wasted on the act of attempting to excrete the contents of your stomach. Mind blowing. She rose above it by calming herself down, thinking about the preparation and hard work she had put in. She didn't panic, and that's why the "nice feeling of calm" brought her adrenalin levels back to the middle, back to the spot at which she could perform at her best. Then she went out and did it.

So if you are hyper-aroused and freaking out, modulating adrenalin and fear is about restoring some calm, some logic back into the situation. If you are hypo (under)-aroused, then you need to build your energy levels and focus. There are many techniques to achieve this:

- self-talk like Libby did
- meditation
- breathing
- strong positive memories can be visual, auditory or kinaesthetic feelings
- a favourite song can pump you up or calm you down
- other external stimuli such as other people, the finish line itself, competitors, and so forth

No single thing works for everyone, be sure of that. Just find something that works for you. For me, the song *More Than a Feeling* by the American band Boston takes my energy levels to exactly the spot I need. I don't even need to hear the song being played; I can hear it play in my mind. Just a bit of the chorus or the wailing guitar riff can make me feel happy, excited, pumped and ready to go every time.

What is it for you? What are the things that can help reduce fear, increase energy, reduce adrenalin in your life? Take 56.73seconds – Libby's gold medal winning time in the 100m butterfly – to write it down in the MY THINGS TO WORK ON section of this book. Go on, do it now!

Feel the Fear

The last word on this topic belongs to a very famous book on fear by Susan Jeffers. Titled <u>Feel the Fear and Do It Anyway</u>, the book explores ways in which we can overcome fear and anxiety by im-mersing ourselves in what we fear. First published in 1987, and having sold over two million copies worldwide, it was, and remains, somewhat of a phenomenon in the self-help industry.

Whilst I appreciate the risk of oversimplifying something, here is my take on Feel the Fear:

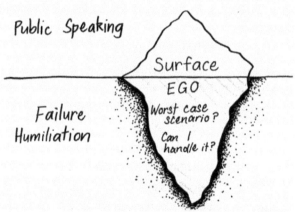

Think of fear like an iceberg. On the surface, we think, "wow what a big iceberg," but you ain't seen nothin' yet. Underneath the surface of the water is mass of iceberg many times larger than what you see on the surface.

Surface level fears – like the fear of speaking in public – seem large. People who suffer this fear will avoid any and every opportunity to get up in front of a group, and many eventually shake off their mortal coils successfully having dodged and manoeuvred around their fear of public speaking.

Susan asks us to go below the surface, deeper into what is really behind our fear, in this example, the fear of public speaking. When we go beneath the surface, we find that it is usually to do with our sense of self, our ego. As the Skyhooks said, "ego is not a dirty word". Ego is our impression of ourselves, and for the fear of public speaking, an ego-related fear usually means fear of failure, humiliation or rejection.

I like to employ the "why" technique to uncover people's deeper beliefs and fears. It goes something like this:

Me:	What do you fear?
Them:	Public speaking
Me:	Why?
Them:	Not sure, I just do not like speaking in public.
Me:	OK. What is it about speaking in public that bothers you?
Them:	I don't want them to laugh at me?
Me:	What's wrong with that?
Them:	I would be embarrassed

TRUE FEAR: HUMILIATION

After this true, ego-related fear has been uncovered, Susan eloquently asks us to do two things to get over it: imagine the **worst-case scenario**, and then ask yourself **whether you can handle it**.

If you have ever experienced a public speaking course run by Toastmasters, you will know what Susan means. I recall doing Toastmasters when I was at school, and I was the only child in the group. All of the others were very nervous adults, possibly coerced or under duress to "fix" their fear of public speaking.

After everyone had registered and taken their seat, the course convenor closed the door. There was something very symbolic in that simple act. He then welcomed the group and pointed to someone randomly in the group and asked them to step up in front of the group. He asked them to speak about green tree frogs for seven minutes.

This very flummoxed course participant slowly rose from her chair, as if she was entering a haunted house. She turned to face the audience and she was shaking visibly. She ummed and ahhed for 30 seconds and said the word tree frog a few times. Everyone in the room felt sick – for her and for themselves as they knew they would be up soon.

Then I noticed the exodus. A few people had already up and left. Before two minutes were over, seven people had left the room, never to return. I understand that at the time – more than 25 years ago – the average attrition rate in the short course within the first hour was approximately 25%. One quarter of people so filled with fear that they could not stay to fix their fear. I am not sure if the process for Toastmasters has changed, and I hope it has not.

After everyone remaining has a go at talking for a significant amount of time on a topic they know nothing about, then the convenor returns. The message is simple – you have just experienced the worst case scenario. You failed miserably, you looked foolish, your skills were poor...and you are still here. You survived.

The course then went on to show us how to plan and structure a speech, deliver with confidence and improving our speaking skills. We were all significantly better for it when we left. Of course we were. We were up-skilled and coached, but mostly we were shown how to conquer our fear. We experienced worst case scenario and we handled it. It wasn't nice to experience, but we kept going.

For me this was the key message of Susan's book. After we have recognised the true fear, and if we can honestly come to terms with the worst case scenario and the fact that we can handle it, fear dissipates. It just does. I would strongly recommend this technique for people with a fear of public speaking. Read the book, employ the technique and remove your fear so you can perform at your very best.

Chapter 5: Removing Brain Blinkers

"No! Do or do not. There is no try."

Luke's X-wing fighter was firmly wedged in the swamp. He had a premonition that his friends were in dire trouble and had made the decision to stop his Jedi training early in order to save his friends. Yoda – Luke's Jedi master – opposed the idea, but allowed Luke to make the decision, so Luke started to lift his X-wing out of the swamp using the Force.

Although it squirmed and jolted a little, Luke could not do it. Yoda beckoned him to do it again, and Luke said he would try.

Then Yoda spoke the immortal quote you read on the previous page.

You probably know what happened after that. Luke failed yet again, and Yoda stepped in and brought the fighter out in an incredible scene. Luke walked around his fighter in sheer amazement. Tiny little Yoda moved this massive fighter plane out of a swamp. Luke says:

"I can't believe it."

Yoda retorts with the quote of the century:

"That is why you fail."

Do or Do Not

I have always wished I were a Jedi. I wanted the light sabres, the Force, the prestige, and to sit on the Jedi council and make decisions to help the universe.

I like to think that some of George Lucas' messages in Star Wars have helped me over the many years I was a fan. Be at one with the universe. Control your anger so the Dark Side cannot tempt you.

Now that we have explored the ways in which Brain Blinkers can prevent us from achieving our best, we need to do something about it. Not try, but do.

There is an important caveat: this book is far from the be all and end all on this subject. As I explained in the introduction to this book, <u>Brain Blinkers</u> is my way of sharing ideas, theories and real life examples that have helped shape my life and the lives of others I know. What I am about to put forward is simply **one method** of removing mental barriers, and certainly not the only way.

We can remove Brain Blinkers both consciously and subconsciously. These techniques, tools and processes include, but are not limited to:

- Cognitive behavioural therapy
- Counselling
- Psychiatric/psychological consultation
- Visualisation techniques
- NLP
- Hypnosis
- Other religious and non-religious processes, for example, chakras

The most important aspect about all of this: **DO SOMETHING.**

The A.C.I.D Test

I took chemistry for one year in high school. I remember the "acid test" referred to a test to deter-

86

mine whether a metal is actual gold. Nowadays it has a much broader context and application.

To go through an "acid test" is to evaluate something thoroughly, to put something through its paces, and to test it to find out what it is really worth.

That is why I chose it as an acronym for how we can remove our own Brain Blinkers. It requires rigour, tenacity, strength. It requires commitment, and a little bit of old-fashioned "elbow grease."

Be AWARE That You Have a Brain Blinker

I truly hope you spent some time filling in the page at the back of this book titled MY THINGS TO WORK ON. If by now you have filled in a few things about your own limiting beliefs, self-sabotage techniques and fears, then you have completed the A in the A.C.I.D test. Congratulations.

Being aware of your Brain Blinker means you are more than half way to removing it. I had no idea I harboured an unconscious bias against Ford until I was 34 years old. You might have discovered something about your behaviour, beliefs and thoughts that you never really knew. If so, this is simply fantastic.

Remember that most people live their lives in their cages and never bother to pry open the door.

The trick from now on is to *continue* to be aware. Here's how:

- Keep your mind open
- Ask others for feedback
- Share the Brain Blinkers terminology with them
- Listen intently to people
- Document areas of your life needing improvement and what might lie at the core of the problem

CHALLENGE the Brain Blinker

After recognising the Brain Blinker, you must challenge it. Ask yourself these questions about the limiting belief or self-sabotage technique:

- Does this belief/behaviour make sense for me now?
- Does it help me?
- Is it something I want to change?
- Do I want this belief or behaviour to continue?

Sometimes, a limiting belief or method of self-sabotage makes sense. For example, you might have been brought up to believe people of other races or religions are not to be trusted – it makes sense that you still believe it, but it may – and should – be something you want to change.

You need to draw an imaginary line in the sand.

The decision needs to be affirmative and clear – change it or do not change it. There is no "try."

After you challenge the Brain Blinker in theory, a very important balancing act needs to occur. We have all had times when we have decided to do something but not followed through with it. Losing weight, achieving fitness, and learning a language are all very common examples of this phenomena.

We need to balance the benefit of *not* changing with the benefit of changing. Think of it as a set of scales: whichever side is heavier ultimately will win.

We need to consider this over both the short and long term in order to truly kick-start a change in our beliefs. I will use the example of smoking to highlight the importance of this part of the A.C.I.D test.

Let us assume that this very intelligent smoker is now aware of his Brain Blinker – his limiting belief simply is that he cannot give up smoking. He tried in the past and it did not work, so therefore it will not work now. Can you see a few Brain Blinkers in action here? First is the limiting belief that he cannot give up smoking. Secondly, he is engaging in self-sabotage by negatively forecasting the outcome.

Let us also assume he really does *want* to quit and look at his table:

	Benefits of not quitting	Benefits of quitting
Short Term	• The buzz of smoking • Habit • No craving	• Financial • Smell better • Feel better
Long Term	• Socially accepted	• Better health

What you put into this table should be not up to anyone other than you, as you are the person who wants to change. Note opinions like "socially accepted" appear in the table above. I personally do not believe this, but my opinion has nothing to do with this fictitious smoker. It is fundamentally required that the person doing the changing OWNS this table, otherwise it is a waste of time, and the attempt to change also becomes a waste of time.

After you honestly and frankly complete this table, weigh the benefits on an imaginary set of scales. Which side is heavier, to change or not to change? That is the question.

Move forward to the next part only if you can honestly say that the scales favour changing.

IMAGINE what's Possible

The third step in this cognitive process is an act of visualisation. We need to imagine what things will be like after the change occurs. What would be possible? What feels and looks good?

Elite sportspeople have used this technique for many years. Some athletes visualise crossing a finish line in first place and soaking in all of the different emotions and senses that come with it: the sound of a crowd going wild, the burning feeling of an outstretched arm as it crosses the line, the smell of liniment and sweat. This technique allows the emotional part of our brain to wallow in what might be, because emotions are a powerful motivator.

Think back to the smoking example. Which one of the following statements is more motivating and therefore more likely to assist change?

- I will be $50 a week better off.
- With an extra $50 in my pocket each week, I could afford to take out that loan on a small boat. I could finally get out on Sydney harbour and enjoy one of the world's most beautiful harbours from the water.

Did you get a better visual from number two? I hope so. Imagine what would be possible, and imagine the emotional impact of your change on your life. As Ali G would say, you need to keep it real because the conscious brain likes a bit of reality, but make it creative, make it lively, and paint a picture that engages your subconscious mind.

After you have that visualisation, reproduce it. Print it out and put it somewhere you will see it often. You have probably seen work desks or offices where people have placed a picture of a holiday destination as a constant reminder. You want to do that with some aspect of your change – make it quirky and fun if you like, but most importantly make it something to which you aspire.

DO It!

Do not talk about it, don't discuss it, and please don't hold a meeting over it. Do everything and anything you must to make it happen.

When I deliver the Brain Blinkers talk around the world, this part of the A.C.I.D test is where I am always amazed at the variety of tools and techniques people use to do things. Here are some ideas:

- Find someone who has made the same change and get advice on what to do and how to do it
- Put EVERYTHING in your diary or journal. Make sure it gets into your busy schedule because if it is there, the chance of getting it done is
- Set the goal and plan for its success
- Enrol in the course, buy the book, invest in the learning
- Appoint a sentinel, someone who will help you on your journey of change and will look after you

Finally

I do not wish you good luck; rather I wish good implementation and good application. Like anyone who has done anything in life, it comes down to what you do, not what you know. The knowledge in this book is useless if it is not applied, and the only person in the world who can do that is you.

May the force be with you.

MY THINGS TO WORK ON

General
Issues

Limiting
Beliefs

Self-Sabotage

Fears

The A.C.I.D Test

Be **AWARE**.

Write down the
Brain Blinker in your
own words.

CHALLENGE the
Brain Blinker. Do
you need it? Do you
want it?

What's the benefit of
holding on to it,
versus the benefit of
removing it? Which
side is heavier?

IMAGINE what's
possible without this
Brain Blinker.

How do you feel?
What does life look
like? What could you
do?

DO IT.

What action will you
take RIGHT NOW to
change your
thinking?

RECOMMENDED READING

Awaken the Giant Within..................Anthony Robbins

Change Your Thinking............................Sarah Edelman

Feel the Fear and Do It Anyway...............Susan Jeffers

How I Raised Myself from Failure to Success in

Selling...Frank Bettger

Influence..Robert Cialdini

Introducing NLP.................... O'Connor & Seymour

POP! Stand Out in Any Crowd...............Sam Horn

Six Thinking Hats...............................Edward De Bono

The Brain That Changes Itself............Norman Doidge

The Mechanism of the Mind.............Edward De Bono

The Oz Principle............Connors, Smith & Hickman

The Power of Your Subconscious Mind.............Joseph
Murphy